# Finches

## ...as a hobby

### by Dennis Kelsey-Wood

**SAVE-OUR-PLANET SERIES**

**T.F.H. Publications, Inc.**
1 T.F.H. Plaza • Third & Union Aves. • Neptune, NJ 07753

## Contents

**Photographs and Illustrations:** Michael Gilroy, Dr. M. Vriends, R. & V. Moat, T. Tilford, Horst Mayer, Michael Defreitas, John Quinn, Dan Martin, Harry V. Lacey, Paul Kwast, Keith Hindwood, W.A. Starika, H.Schrempp, Horst Bielfeld, Vogelpark Walsrode.

Distributed in the UNITED STATES to the Pet Trade by T.F.H. Publications, Inc., One T.F.H. Plaza, Neptune City, NJ 07753; distributed in the UNITED STATES to the Bookstore and Library Trade by National Book Network, Inc. 4720 Boston Way, Lanham MD 20706; in CANADA to the Pet Trade by H & L Pet Supplies Inc., 27 Kingston Crescent, Kitchener, Ontario N2B 2T6; Rolf C. Hagen Ltd., 3225 Sartelon Street, Montreal 382 Quebec; in CANADA to the Book Trade by Macmillan of Canada (A Division of Canada Publishing Corporation), 164 Commander Boulevard, Agincourt, Ontario M1S 3C7; in the United Kingdom by T.F.H. Publications, PO Box 15, Waterlooville PO7 6BQ; in AUSTRALIA AND THE SOUTH PACIFIC by T.F.H. (Australia), Pty. Ltd., Box 149, Brookvale 2100 N.S.W., Australia; in NEW ZEALAND by Brooklands Aquarium Ltd. 5 McGiven Drive, New Plymouth, RD1 New Zealand; in Japan by T.F.H. Publications, Japan—Jiro Tsuda, 10-12-3 Ohjidai, Sakura, Chiba 285, Japan; in SOUTH AFRICA by Multipet Pty. Ltd., P.O. Box 35347, Northway, 4065, South Africa. Published by T.F.H. Publications, Inc.

Manufactured in the United States of America by T.F.H. Publications, Inc.

# Introduction

Black Hooded and White Headed Nuns are among the most familiar finches of the nun, or mannikin, group.

The keeping of small birds in cages dates back many centuries, in fact, so far back, that no one really knows when this pastime first commenced. The great appeal to those who first placed birds into a cage was no doubt because of either their wonderful song, or their vivid colors, or both. With the passage of time the mere keeping of avians was not enough for some, they wanted to breed them as well. When this happened, aviculture, in its truest sense, began.

For many centuries, and sadly still so today, small birds were retained in very tiny cages. During the early

years of the 18th century a certain Duc de Nivernais hit on the idea of an "original device" for allowing birds much more freedom than had previously been granted to them. The device was of course, the aviary. The Duke covered a small wood near his home with fine netting and released many birds into it. The idea caught on in a big way. Within just a few years the homes of nobility were hardly complete without at least one large aviary.

By the 19th century the social changes that swept Europe in the wake of the Industrial Revolution meant that the middle, and later the working classes, were keeping all manner of birds in both cages and aviaries. Initially, the less opulent working classes kept only indigenous species. But as the 20th century got underway prosperity allowed more exotic birds to filter down to just about all levels of society.

The growing popularity of aviculture resulted with the formation of many bird societies dedicated to propagating certain groups of birds, including foreign birds. Following the end of

The sizes of outdoor aviaries vary enormously. The most popular size for small town gardens is about 10 or 12 feet in length, 6 feet wide, and about 7 feet high.

World War II the keeping of pet birds became a craze largely brought about by the omnipresent budgerigar. However, many years before the arrival of this little Australian parrot, finches and canaries had been the mainstay of aviculture.

Today, the hobby of birdkeeping has expanded to become an enormous pastime which, accounting for food and accessories, turns over an abundance of capital.

**DEFINING FINCH-LIKE BIRDS**

In the strict sense of zoological definition, a finch is any member of the family Fringillidae, which itself is a member of the very large order of avians known as Passeriformes, the perching birds. Bird keepers tend to keep birds not so much based on their zoological standing, but rather on the way they feed. Finches are essentially seedeaters, so any small bird that can be reared on a seed diet is commonly regarded as being a finch-like bird, and will appear in a mixed collections of these.

Actually popular birdkeeping terms, such as hardbills (having a beak capable of cracking nuts or seeds), and softbills (those that live mainly on soft-foods, fruits, and insects),

are rather misleading. Rarely are these terms mutually exclusive. Many finches, including hardbills, consume quite a lot of insects and fruit during the breeding period, while likewise, a number of "softbills" readily eat seed. As long as these realities are appreciated, popular terminology is quite acceptable.

For the purposes of this book the term "finch-like" is restricted to finches, waxbills, weavers, and sparrows. You could easily widen the scope of finch-like birds to embrace many other types, such as the buntings, but from a beginner's viewpoint the ones cited contain the vast majority of easily kept, and readily available, small, seed-eating birds.

The text is basic. It does not attempt to go into great detail on any one subject and is filled with sound, general advice. What follows are the essentials of

Like its close relative the Lavender Waxbill, the Black Tailed Lavender Waxbill is difficult to sex; but if the birds are mature, females show less vividness and less extensive red on the rump and ventral areas.

Java Rice Birds are quite aggressive when kept among birds of other species, it is recommended that one pair be kept with other birds of the same size for breeding purposes.

being able to purchase and maintain a number of finch-like birds either by species, or in a mixed collection. Once you are underway, or have decided which species to keep, it is advised to obtain one or more detailed works that are appropriate to your particular needs. In the final chapter of the book a number of popular species are discussed. The descriptions will provide you with a general overview of the species. The many photographs throughout this book will give you a much better idea of what they look like than mere words could ever do. If the advice given is followed, and combined with a common sense approach, you will find that the finch-like birds are truly delightful avians to own as pets, to breed, and to exhibit. Many are very low priced when compared with other birds, and their upkeep costs are minimal. Some have a pleasant song, and many are very colorful.

Finch-like birds will not annoy your neighbors with raucous voices, as might parrot-like birds, nor will they destroy a planted aviary. This means that you can really create an esthetically pleasing outdoor enclosure for them. Alternatively, they can be kept and bred indoors. Another advantage of most birds within this group is that they will happily coexist alongside birds of similar size. Given proper care, members of the finch-like group may live for up to twenty years, though a life span of half this should be regarded as being more typical. Over all, you could not find another group of avians that offer so much for so little an outlay.

# Stock Selection

Before venturing out to purchase one or more finch-like birds make sure that you have adequate housing waiting for them upon returning home. The type of housing needed will be influenced by the stock you plan to keep. Therefore, it is appropriate to discuss this first.

**PET, BREEDING, OR SHOW?**

Finches can be purchased as either pet, breeding, or show birds. The difference between these three types lies essentially in respect to their quality. This also greatly influences the source of their supply. Their cost is determined by their quality, age, and a few other factors. A pet finch need not be of show or breeding quality, meaning that it may display some minor faults that would be undesirable

Bullfinch. Bullfinches get on well in an aviary with other species. They thrive on the feedings of greens as well as softfoods.

Orange Bishop Weaver. When kept in a cage and the proper food is not supplied, the orange-red color of this bird is apt to fade to a pale tone.

in the other types. This could be in respect to the depth of color or the markings, depending on the species. Some finches have exhibition standards, others do not. In those with standards, color and markings are critical factors. As long as a pet finch is a typical member of its species, and is a healthy specimen, quality is not important—unless you want especially fine examples. Breeder finches do not necessarily have to be good enough to be exhibition birds, but if sound in color and markings, they could produce excellent offspring. Much depends on whether or not you wish to breed for exhibition stock, or just for fun. Show birds of course need to be of high visual standards with no obvious defects either to anatomy or to color markings. It does not follow that good show birds are automatically good breeding birds, because good breeding birds are dependent on genotype.

There are two types of show birds, the carefully bred (those that are likely to pass on virtuous features to future generations) and the super looking bird that came about more by random nature of the ways genes combine (luck) rather than

Society Finch. No two Society Finches are exactly alike in their mottled pattern. Coloring varies from pure white to dark chocolate brown.

by careful breeding. This bird may or may not pass on its visual quality. To fully understand this aspect you are advised to read a number of general books on genetics. If you wish to be a breeder/ exhibitor you should also study the show standard of the species in question.

## WHAT AGE IS BEST?

For whatever reason you wish to be a finch owner it is best to purchase the bird when it is a youngster, ideally almost straight from the nest. Once a finch has passed through its first full molt, which is anytime after it is two or more months old, it is impossible to estimate its age, unless it has been banded with a year engraved. A young bird will clearly have a long life span ahead of it, and if exhibition is in its future, its potential winning years will be while it is young. Likewise, hens are most productive during their early years, thereafter, the number of eggs laid start to fall. However, if you wish to make a quick start as a breeder, there would be merit in obtaining quality 1-2 year old proven breeders. Such birds are slightly more expensive if they are any good.

## WHICH SEX IS BEST?

A male bird is a more preferred choice among purchasing a finch as a pet for two reasons. First, for those finches that have a melodious song, only the males sing. Secondly, the male is usually more vividly colored than the female. If you plan to be a breeder or exhibitor then the choice between the sexes is really not important; indeed a breeder will need both.

When birds display a visual difference between the sexes they are known as being sexually dimorphic. A variation on this is when the male displays what is termed "nuptial plumage". In these species the male sports colorful plumage during the breeding period, and perhaps extra long tail feathers as well.

### THE MATTER OF HEALTH

The number one priority, in obtaining any pet, is health. This would appear to be obvious advice yet it is surprising just how many beginners go out and acquire birds that are clearly displaying signs of poor condition. If you plan to breed birds, remember that health embraces not only what you can immediately see, but what you cannot. This means that traits such as parenthood, fertility, and resistance to disease are extremely important. The only way you can gain knowledge of these with respect to the birds you purchase is if detailed (and honest) breeding

records have been maintained. The extent of the poor health cannot always be ascertained by the physical signs because these may indicate a minor condition, such as a chill, as well as a major disease. Given this fact, one cannot afford to take a chance with any but the healthiest individuals. The following are the obvious signs of ill health:

1. The feathers of any bird should appear immaculate. An odd broken feather is not a problem, it will be replaced at the next molt. Areas of missing feathers, be these on the head, wings, or body, are indicative of a problem. Missing head feathers are invariably the result of being plucked by other

Red Avadavat. The Avadavat is unusual in that it has a seasonal change of plumage. Outside the breeding season, it may be difficult to distinguish the out-of-color cock from the hen shown here.

The St. Helena Waxbill is one of the most popular of the waxbill family. It is a very hardy bird and a fairly free breeder. The St. Helena proves to be rather aggressive during breeding and is very territorial.

birds, and will regrow once the "pluckers" are removed. It is safest to select birds displaying tight to the body feathers with a sheen.

2. The eyes of a healthy bird are round and very clear. Any form of liquid discharge, cloudiness, or half closed eyes, indicate a problem.

3. The fleshy cere area above the beak should not be swollen, nor should there be any discharge from the nostrils.

4. The beak should fit neatly, the two mandibles meeting such that they are nicely aligned. Cracked, pitted, crusty, or misaligned beaks indicate a problem.

5. The breast bone of a bird should be well covered with flesh. If it is protruding, chances are it is "going light". This is the outward sign of a number of problems that are not easily overcome. One is that the bird has suffered from an inadequate diet deficient in certain vitamins.

6. The vent area should be clean with no signs of staining. This would suggest a present or recent illness.

7. The scales on the legs should lay flat. Raised scales indicate a parasitic mite problem.

8. There should be three forward and one backward facing toes. A missing forward toe is not a major problem for a pet bird, but would be undesirable in a show finch.

9. An ill bird tends to sit as far away as possible from other active birds. Its feathers will be fluffed and its head drooped forward. It will be resting with both feet grasping the perch.

When sleeping, a healthy bird does so on one leg and with its head turned to rest on the back of its neck. A very ill bird flutters to the floor because it does not have the strength to hold the perch. However, young birds that are nervous or frightened will also seek refuge on the floor. Only with experience can you determine the difference between nervousness and ill health totally from behavioral actions.

**WHERE TO PURCHASE STOCK**

There are many sources that sell finch-like birds. These include private breeders, pet shops, and bird farms. These three sources offer advantages depending on your needs and location. For a finch of average quality, that is to be a pet or ornamental aviary bird, the pet shop is both convenient and a good source. It will be able to supply virtually all your likely needs, as well as good advice. Bird farms are able to offer a wide range of stock in those species that are difficult to attain. They may also stock a number of specialty products that your local pet shop may not keep on its shelves. If you

European Goldfinch. The sexes of the European Goldfinch are very similar; but the general conception regarding the distinction is that males are more red on the head, are slightly larger, and have a more pointed beak.

Dybowski's Twinspot. Important features of this bird are the white spots on a black background on the lower chest extending to the abdomen and through the flanks; and a broad swath of deep crimson starting on the broad mantle and covering the back, rump, and upper tail coverts.

require quality breeding or exhibition stock, the private breeder is the obvious source (especially in respect to the domestic, or nearly so, species). "Domestic" refers to birds which are very popular and are largely bred under captive conditions. Such species include all Australian finches which have not been allowed to be exported since 1959. Java sparrows, various manikins, and a growing number of other Asian and African finches are now being bred on a regular basis under captive conditions. Such birds are preferable to wild caught

individuals because they are invariably hardier, much healthier, and quite used to life in a captive environment. If you wish to specialize in color varieties of a given species, such as Zebra Finches, Gouldians, and their like, the private breeder is the source. It is important that you know what the genetic makeup is of the stock you buy. You do not want to waste much time and money trying to find this out through breeding results. Essentially, in respect to the health conditions of the birds. Regardless of whether a breeder, pet shop, or bird farm, the

Dark Fire Finch. There are several subspecies of the Dark Fire Finch, differing only slightly from one another. This species is one of the group of reddish African finches that occasionally has become available to finch fanciers.

supplier must be reliable. The cages should be clean with no suggestion that the perches or floors are caked in fecal matter. The water container should have clean water in it, and the seed dishes should contain seed, never be empty, or obviously full of husks. The birds should not be overcrowded. The general cleanliness of the establishment should satisfy you that hygiene is not a foreign word to the seller!

**BIRD SHOWS**

A potential finch-like keeper who goes ahead and buys birds without visiting at least two bird shows is doing themselves a great disfavor. Any foreign bird exhibition displays all of the more popular species—as well as a number of the lesser seen finch-like birds. No better idea of what good condition is all about can be had than at a show because show birds must be in super feather and good general health. You will be able to ask any questions you may have and be confident that the answer is truthful and based on experience. At the larger shows there are, apart from the breeders, both pet shops and bird farms selling stock, as well as all of the many accessories now available to aviculturalists. The show is thus potentially a one stop shopping window to the entire hobby. Shows are advertised in various avicultural magazines.

Owl Finch. The Owl Finch is a fairly long-lived bird, but is not too free a breeder under captive conditions. In the wild it breeds quite readily.

### THE COST OF STOCK

The cost of stock depends on a number of factors, especially in regards to quality. There are aspects that you may not be familiar with which are worthy of mention. There are two types of "pairs". One simply means two birds, the other means a male and female. With sexually monomorphic species, birds are often sold as two birds, it being pot luck if they are of the same sex or not. A true pair within this type of species is rather costly. A proven pair is even more costly, especially if they are of one of the less popular species. "Proven" means that they have already produced offspring. The term "compatible pair" simply means the pair gets on well together, not that they have bred. Full colored pairs in those species which the male displays nuptial plumage are more costly than when out of color. Single hens in certain species are more costly than males. Mutational colors always command higher prices than the normal wild-type color patterns. The more rare the mutation, the more expensive it will be. This, however, does not mean it is more visually pleasing, just more rare. When you add in the aspect of quality, with regards to breeding or show stock, the total combinations that effect price are considerable. All of this behooves you to know exactly what sort of stock you want, then obtain a number of price quotations so that you can establish what is average for the type of stock you are looking for. There are rarely bargains in finch-like birds, so if a price seems very low to you compared to the norm, work on the basis that it is what it is, meaning its price is a reflection of its quality.

Orange Cheeked Waxbills are a favorite bird among beginners. They are very attractive, inexpensive, and quite hardy. Another plus among this species is that they are very prolific.

# Cages & Aviaries

Finch-like birds are probably the easiest birds to accommodate in respect to their housing. Unlike parrot-like birds, finches do not destroy the wood framing of cages, and aviaries, perches, and nest boxes, or plants that are featured in the accommodation. Further, their small size means housing can be more moderate, thus less costly to erect, both in relation to the amount of materials needed and substance.

## CAGES

The range of commercially made finch cages available now is greater than ever before. Some are excellent, others are a waste of hard earned money. The needs of your finch's housing are simple: it should be as large as possible and designed to make cleaning simple. Beyond these needs all else is essentially decoration.

Size: The minimum cage size should be 77x38x38cm (30x15x15in) for a pair of small finches. I do stress that this is the smallest size—the larger the cage, the far better off the birds will be. Length is always more important than height for any bird species, and especially so for finches because they fly back and forth, not up and down. Because of this, ornate, tall, round cages are definitely unsuitable for your pet. Likewise, a number of the small cages that are marketed for finches are also inadequate unless they

The box style cage is most often used by breeders and has changed very little over the years.

are purely a temporary form of accommodation, or of course unless you are purchasing a show or hospital cage.

Owners have been using undersized cages for small birds for no other reason than invariably all that was on sale for far too many years. This is no longer the case. Much larger and better cages are now being produced. Larger cages are more expensive, but necessary if you want your pet to have a spacious home. An alternative to costly metal cages is a double or triple breeder wooden cage that can be painted to your desired color. This type allows your pets to actually fly from one end to the other, rather than flutter, which is the reality of smaller cages.

Another option is to purchase low cost, large, indoor flights that come mounted on castors (wheels) so that they can be easily moved around. The wire bars of a finch cage are closer together than those for larger birds, and the doors usually slide upward. This is safer in catching the birds, as opposed to a door that opens downward.

Furnishings: A cage requires several seed vessels or dispensers, a water container, and a dish

Pintailed Whydah. The very attractive Pintailed Whydah is very aggressive to small birds during their "in color" phase. It is best that they be housed with other birds that can fend for themselves.

for softfoods (fruits and or proprietary brand soft-foods). Seed cups can be of the open dish variety or automatic dispensers. A word of caution, automatic seed dispensers can jam and therefore must be checked several times a day. Flomatic water dispensers are superior to open cups because the water is kept free of dust, fecal fouling, and seed husks.

Cages should feature at least two perches, more if the cage is large. There are many styles and sizes of perches available such as round, triangular, and square. Perches with differing diameters placed in the cage are best for your finch's feet—they

Many finch keepers believe that breeding finches is best accomplished with a bird room. Pairs separated into cages are free of disturbance from other avian companions.

provide variable exercise for them. Doweling is the most popular choice of wood, but plastic perches are also available. An alternative to commercial perches is to cut lengths of fruit (except cherry) or other tree branches such as willow. These are

natural and easily replaced at no cost. Fittings are available to hold them in place in the cage.

Cage Floor: There are two potential ways that the floor of the cage is made. One is where a sliding drawer is fitted to facilitate ease of cleaning, the other

is where the bottom of the cage can be separated from the top for the removal of feces and debris. The drawer type is the more popular, but it is a matter of personal preference as to which is regarded as best. To protect the floor you can line it with paper for ease of cleaning.

Cage Stands: Avoid any stand that is not really solid or that can be easily knocked over. It is better to place the cage on a firm surface, such as a wide shelf, table, or similar unit.

Breeder Cage Separations: There are a wide range of cage separations produced for breeders. These are light and airy and can be purchased in sections so that more can be easily added when the need

arises. Many come complete with small wheels so they are readily moved to make cleaning under and behind more convenient.

**PLACEMENT OF PET CAGES**

Finches are hardy little birds, but because of their small size and rapid metabolism they can quickly deteriorate if they do become ill. A major factor that easily induces problems is subjecting them to rapid changes in temperature. The placement of the cage is therefore a matter of importance. It should never be situated in a risk of

Strawberry Finch. Strawberry Finches are difficult to breed; but if proper conditions are provided, many become surprisingly prolific.

The size of cage for your finch depends on the type of finch you plan to keep. Some finch species are quite nervous and require a lot of room to fly.

draft—such as opposite a door or near a window. It should never be sited where it is subjected to long periods of direct sunlight. Birds enjoy the sunshine, but should always be able to retreat into a shaded area of the cage. If your home is centrally heated, do not place the cage near a vent, this creates rapid temperature changes as it comes on and goes off. Try to locate the cage so that it is eye level or slightly below this. Birds feel more secure kept at a higher level, and it also saves you from having to stoop to see your

pets and attend chores. Placing the birds down low also stresses them easily.

**AVIARIES**

There is no doubt that by far the best way to keep a collection of finch-like birds is in a planted aviary. In this way, they can be seen at their very best as they go about their day to day lives in a semblance of normality. In a cage, this is not possible to do unless it is of the large indoor flight type. Birds derive the benefits of fresh air, sunshine, and rain in an aviary.

Finches are highly social birds. Species can be mixed without problems as

The Zebra Finch is the most popular and readily available Australian Finch. It is quite accustomed to living in smaller cages and breeds easily.

Gouldian Finch. The male of this species is the more beautiful sex. Females are duller and paler additions of the male particularly in regard to the greatly reduced intensity of the chest.

long as certain aspects are given due consideration. The aviary should be large enough to allow each species, or pair of birds, ample room to avoid other species if they so wish. This becomes vital once pairs settle down to breed. During breeding season the character of birds changes dramatically. They tend to become aggressive towards other species that they ordinarily get on well with. The factors that create disputes are usually with regard to nesting sites, nest boxes, and the distance between these. Each pair requires its own territory. The size of this area is not easily determined, so the way to proceed is to allow ample space and not risk overstocking the aviary. Through observation and experience you can determine how much space each pair needs, and add or remove accordingly. Bear in mind that an aviary represents a total ecosystem for your birds. This system embraces a

Millet in spray form is natural for finches, as the relish with which they consume it proves. In addition to nutritional value, it also provides healthful activity, since it demands more effort than picking a seed from a dish. Photo courtesy Rolf C. Hagen Corp.

society of birds that get to know each other, regardless of their species. The peace and harmony within the society can be disrupted by the addition of aggressive individuals or pairs. How the birds interact with each other should be monitored. Remember, the ecosystem created within an aviary is not at all natural. Many of the finches in the aviary normally would not live together because they come from differing countries and environments. All of this means you must be observant and apply common sense to the ways you manage the ecosystem you are creating.

Alternatives to the mixed aviary collection are a species aviary, or an aviary in which the birds will be bred in pairs. The species aviary is advantageous because you can commence a colony with a number of birds of unknown sexes. The laws of average are such that you should get at least a few of each. Once birds have paired, remove the unpaired birds. Some species are more likely to breed within a colony

rather than in pairs. Breeding birds in pairs enables you to have smaller aviaries, but more of them because you will wish to control which birds mate with each other. The only way you can achieve this objective is by placing single pairs in their own aviary, in cages, or indoor flights.

**THE TYPICAL AVIARY**

There are a number of ways an aviary can be designed. An aviary can be square, round, octagonal, or rectangular. It may form part of a line of similar aviaries, all of which connect to a shelter or birdroom that runs along the back of the flights, or it

may be a display aviary which runs across your line of vision as you approach it. The term aviary is therefore defined for our purposes as a unit that contains a flight, a shelter, and a storage or working area.

The choice of style is influenced by your objectives, be this for breeding, or simply for a structure that blends in with your garden and contains a mixed collection of attractive finch-like birds. You will no doubt view a number of styles before deciding which is the one for you.

## THE AVIARY SITE

Regardless of style, all aviaries have a common objective: to house birds in such a way that they can be seen to their best advantage, yet managed in a practical and efficient manner. With these needs in mind, the aviary site

Violet Eared Waxbill. Normally, Violet Eared Waxbills are reported to be difficult to maintain in good condition due to sudden unexpected deaths for no apparent reason.

Cordon Bleus are very charming and pretty, and under proper conditions will breed. Breeding successes are dependant upon a number of different factors such as, ample supply of small livefoods, as much seclusion as possible, and a well planted aviary.

requires major considerations. You may not have a choice of sites, but if you do, incorporate as many of the following points into your planning as you can.

1. The flight should face the south as much as possible. This will give the birds the benefit of the early morning sunshine, and longer exposure to this.
2. Avoid sitting the flights under overhanging tree branches. This provides good shade and protection from cold winds, however, it also presents problems such as wild bird droppings, rain drops that fall long after the rain has stopped, insect activity, predators, and falling leaves.
3. Choose high ground in order to avoid the risk of flooding after heavy storms or swollen streams. If need be, build up the site.
4. Choose a site that is reasonably close to your home and in sight of your most lived in rooms.
5. Choose a site that enjoys protection from cold winds and driving rain. If no such site exists, the exposed sides of the flight can be covered with panels of plastic during the worst months, or a protective fence can be erected.
6. Ponder the potential of the site for future expansion. Does it allow for extra flights to be added?
7. Check that the aviary is not placed over sewage, water, or main electric lines that might need repair at some future date.
8. Make inquiries pertaining to local zoning laws. Such laws might influence the number of aviaries you are allowed to have, the number of

birds, and the materials to be used in the aviary. Generally, aviaries built using wood are no problem because they are not regarded as permanent structures. The use of brick might need planning consent or a building permit. Services to the aviary might also be subject to installation regulations. It would also be wise to mention to your neighbors what you plan and assure them that finch-like birds are not noisy.

**THE AVIARY FLIGHT FLOOR**

The aviary floor should be a compromise situation between what is natural and what is hygienic. Earth and grass are clearly natural and esthetically pleasing, but also represent a potential health hazard. The constant droppings of both the aviary and wild birds means that these surfaces can become breeding grounds for pathogens (disease causing organisms). Such floors cannot be cleaned. Gravel is a better choice because it can be raked and hosed. Slabs are even better from the cleaning viewpoint, while concrete is arguably the best of all. By having a concrete or slabbed floor the risk of predators such as mice, rats, weasels,

Red Eared Waxbill. Although the Red Eared Waxbill is quite common, it is a very difficult bird to breed. They usually show a complete disinterest in breeding.

Purple Grenadier. The splendidly colored cock is one of the most admired finches. Although a steady finch, breeding success with this species has not been extensive.

In the realm of sprouted seeds and greens, a pot of growing grasses will entertain and enhance the diet of finches, particularly those kept in cages. Nature's Little Greenhouse from Four Paws offers fresh home-grown greens for birds to enjoy.

foxes or their like, burrowing under the perimeter fence and then gaining access to the birds, is reduced. The concrete should be extended so that it forms a pathway around the entire aviary structure. Do not forget to make provisions for rain and

hosed water to easily leave the flight. A gentle slope away from the shelter will meet this need.

**THE AVIARY FLIGHT**

In order that the flight can withstand gusty winds it should be made using timber of 5x2.5cm (2x1in) or 3.7x3.7cm (1½ x 1½ in) dimensions. Treat it with preservatives to extend its life. To make future repairs easier, it is best to assemble the flight using suitably sized panels. In this way, extensions are made more simple than if weld wire were stretched across a pre-erected frame. The weld wire gauge should be of the order 19G or stronger. The hole size should be maximum 2.5x1.25cm (1x ½ in). This prevents all but the smallest of mice from

entering. The height should be a minimum of 2m (6.5ft). The roof cross members therefore will not spoil your line of vision. The weld wire should be painted with bitumen to mask it to a large degree. From the safety angle, in respect to predatory birds or animals, it is wise to clad the flight frame on both sides. It is also useful to feature a false roof in the flight. The latter can utilize a larger hole size, thus will be less costly (chicken wire would be the most economic material for this, but do not use it on the flight itself as it has a short life and never keeps taut). You may consider placing a reed mat on the roof during very hot periods. This will allow sunlight to be filtered into the flight. It looks neat and provides just the right amount of shade for the birds. Alternatively, in the colder temperate regions, the roof should be partially covered with clear or colored corrugated sheeting. This will provide good protection during inclement weather. During the latter

you could also fit removable sheets of stiff plastic on the most exposed sides.

## THE BIRDROOM SHELTER

Shelter provides overnight refuge for your finches, and it accommodates both cages and indoor flights. It also acts as a storage and work area for you, and therefore should be as large as possible. Think of a generous size, and make it bigger, it will then be the right size! The shelter should allow plenty of light to enter. The use of skylights is a good idea for this because windows take up valuable wall space. The skylights must be able to

Another of the more uncommon African Fire Finches: the Bar Breasted. Here the white spotting found in this group has been elaborated into little bars.

Spice Finch. The Spice Finch is not at all a ready breeder in captivity. It is a quiet bird that can be associated with any small finch provided it is not over crowded.

open to let out hot air. One good sized window can provide a generous amount of air circulation. Be sure all such openings are covered with weld wire in case the glass shatters and birds are flying in the birdroom. Also, the birdroom should be insulated as well as possible. This will keep heating and cooling costs down. It is very important that the bird room be well ventilated. A number of vents located both low and high greatly reduce the risk of bacterial buildup.

**BIRDROOM FURNISHINGS**

It certainly is convenient to have the benefit of

services such as, water, electricity, and sewage in the birdroom. Background heating is also useful, as much for your comforts as for the birds' needs. Never allow the birdroom to become too hot otherwise chills are sure to befall your stock. An ionizer is a very worthwhile investment. It helps keep dust and bacteria to a minimum, and is economical to install and operate. Ample provision of shelves and cupboards, as well as good work surfaces, is a very sound investment. Ensure that a number of spare cages are on hand, as well as one or more exhibition cages. The

The St. Helena has a very active nature which can be seen in its constantly moving tail.

latter are very useful for transporting newly acquired birds even if you have no plans to show your stock.Birds can be startled during the night and will then flutter to the floor where they will stay unless enough light is provided to fly back to a perch. For this reason, a suitable light outside of the aviary is beneficial because it provides the birds with light to see in case they are frightened, and potential thieves will not be likely to approach a building so illuminated. Strong locks should be fitted to all aviary entrance doors to insure against theft.

**PLANNING**

Never rush into the construction or erection of an aviary. The whole project should be planned carefully, and cost is best to estimate before beginning. It is much easier to move things around, or change ideas, at this stage rather than when the project is completed. More pleasure from the hobby will be gained if the accommodation is built according to the standards of the finches as well as your own.

# Feeding Finches

The basic diet for most of the popular finches is comprised of various seeds. However, contrary to popular thought, seeds alone do not constitute a well balanced diet. All finches require other foods, even if only taken in very small quantities. Such foods include fruits, livefoods, wild green plants, and any of the branded softfood mixes that are available.

## GENERAL RECOMMENDATIONS

Before discussing the actual foods we should look at a few general feeding recommendations. Always have time to spend watching your birds feed. Any change in habit (such as displaying no interest in food) might indicate an impending illness. Should this occur, catch the bird and place it into an isolation cage for further observation.

Also, watch to see that each bird is getting its fair share of food. Sometimes more aggressive finches frighten away the timid species or individuals. If this is noticed, the answer is to either have two feeding areas, or more feeders in one area.

Seed Mixtures: Establish which seeds are preferred by your stock so that waste can be minimized. The best way to do so is to supply any but the most popular seeds in separate little crock pots, this way an eating ratio of one seed to another can be established. Your own mixes can then be made, or you may decide to continue feeding the non–maintenance seeds separately. A pet owner with only one or two birds can feed a general finch mixture with a minimal amount of waste. Breeders, on

Pied Java Rice Bird. No two Pied Java Rice Birds are found to have identical markings. A Pied Java may be either predominantly dark or predominantly light.

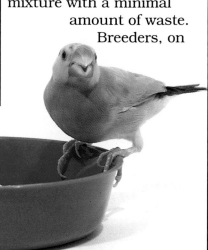

the other hand, should bulk purchase their seeds and make up their own mix, unless, of course, they are happy with a mix prepared by avicultural seed merchants.

Seed Quality and Storage: When you are purchasing loose seed be advised that there is good and bad seed. Seed varies considerably in quality and price, and is dramatically affected by the way it is stored. All this in mind, purchase only quality seed from a reputable source that has selected it with care. As a general guide, any supplier that does a healthy trade in seed should be turning stock over rapidly, therefore, it will be quite fresh.

Seed loses nutrient value unless stored under ideal conditions; dry, cool, and dark. Be sure it is in a sealed container so it is not at risk to rodents or wild birds. Quality seed has a polished look and is free of dust.

Soaked & Sprouted Seeds: Finches generally enjoy both soaked and

A male Purple Grenadier's head and beak are of the same coloration as the Violet Eared Waxbill; but the cheek patch is greatly reduced in size.

sprouted seeds. In this state they are more easily digested and their vitamin content rises. To soak seeds place a small quantity into a shallow dish and cover them with warm water. Place the dish in a darkened cupboard and leave for 24 hours. Remove the seeds and rinse thoroughly before feeding to your birds. To sprout the seeds repeat the forgoing, but after 24 hours rinse and place them on damp paper. Place the dish in a cupboard and leave a further 24-36 hours until small white shoots are seen

Female Purple Grenadiers are far less showy than the males. They are brownish, pale on the underparts, and tinted with chestnut on the head. A white patch surrounds the eye, and white spots are sprinkled on the under-parts. The rump is blue, and the tail is blackish-gray.

when they should be rinsed again and fed to the birds. Do not feed seeds that have developed green shoots, this means they have germinated too long. Inexpensive seed sprouters can be purchased from your pet shop. The feeding life of soaked and sprouted seeds is very short (under 12 hours), so only prepare a sufficient amount for one day at a time, and feed them in a shaded part of the aviary.

Feeding Times: Your birds should have constant access to dry seeds. If open seed vessels are used blow the husks away to make sure there is fresh seed in it, not just husks. Tap automatic dispensers daily to ensure that the seed is falling into the tray— sometimes the outlet on smaller units becomes jammed. All moist foods (softfoods, fruits and green plants) are best fed early in the morning or in the late afternoon. This will keep them fresher than if fed during the hottest part of the day.

Take Care With Greenfoods: Always rinse any plant matter that you give to your birds. This removes residual chemicals from pesticides and motor

fumes. Never gather plants from areas that may have been fouled by dogs, cats or other animals. Be sure frozen greenfoods have been thoroughly thawed. If feeding wild plants, give the entire plant, roots and all, to the birds. Bear in mind that some finches are ground feeders in the wild, others eat from shrubs, bushes, and grasses which they cling to and eat from without problem. The use of clips helps to suspend some wild plants to the aviary netting, but some should be placed on the floor of the shelter as well. Birds should not be allowed to glut on greenfoods. It can be highly dangerous and will result in diarrhea and maybe death. A newly acquired bird that is not accustomed to eating greenfood will consume it as though it is going out of fashion, and then become ill. It is best to supply only small amounts at first and slowly build it up. In this way the digestive systems of your stock can become familiar with the increasing amounts of these foods and

Like the millet spray, the honey stick provides occupation. The additional nutrients incorporated in products such as the Rolf C. Hagen Corp. honey sticks shown here may be helpful in conditioning the finches to breed.

no problems will ensue. In fact, you should apply this policy to all new foods added to the diet.

## FINCH FOODS

Birds do not have any teeth. In order to masticate seeds and other foods they consume variable quantities of minerals in the form of grits of various types. Finch-sized grit must always be available to your birds. Crushed egg– and oyster shells are high in calcium content, which is useful for breeding hens. Charcoal bits also make a useful supplement.

Water: Water is most valuable to birds and should be supplied fresh each day. The quality of water differs from one town to the next, and some is treated with chlorine and chloramines. While these cleansing additives may not harm you, they do affect small creatures, such as finches, over a period of time. Water quality is a matter of importance. Ideally, it should have a neutral pH, or one that is only marginally acidic or alkaline. Spring and distilled waters are best.

Staple Diet Seeds: The two seeds that form the staple diet of finch-like birds are canary and millet. Canary seed is grown in many countries and its price reflects its origins and the quality of the crop. The same is true of millet seeds.

Panicum is the most popular millet. The best way to provide these two seed groups is to mix the seeds of differing countries to be sure that their constituents balance out and that nothing is lacking in the overall mixture. The mix ratio of canary to millet will reflect the preferences of your birds, and their species. It is suggested that you supply a 50/50 mixture of canary/Panicum Millet and adjust this to suit based on observed consumption. Millet can also be purchased on the ear or in the form of sprays. Again, this varies in quality depending on the source. All finches enjoy millet

Zebra Finches mutate and give us different color varieties quite frequently. The Silver and White mutations have been established long enough to be almost as reasonable in price as the Grays.

sprays. Birds will be less inclined to eat other seeds which are higher in nutritional value if these are offered. Moderation in all matters related to

feeding is a sound strategy.

Other Seeds: Canary and millet are rich in carbohydrates (about 58-70%), making them the cheapest energy seed. During the winter and breeding periods other seeds that are rich in proteins and fats such as hemp, niger, maw, and rape also need to be supplied. The proteins and fats in these seeds are essential to breeding birds. They are equally essential to birds recovering from an illness because their energy output potential is greater than canary and millet.

These additional seeds can be supplied as separate mixtures. Through observation, a basic consumed ratio can be established. Bear in mind that maw and rape are especially high in fat content and should be fed sparingly. There are many other seeds, both wild and commercially available, that you can supply to your birds. Never be afraid to experiment because the greater the variety your stock takes, the less chance there is that a

Green Avadavat. the Green Avadavat is easily recognized by its conspicuous blackish-green and white vertical stripes which border the flanks.

valuable constituent will be missing from the diet. Some seeds, such as unsalted peanuts and sunflower, are too large for finch-like birds to cope with. In this case crush the seeds and then allow them to be picked over.

### GREENFOODS

The potential range of greenfoods that can be offered to your stock is virtually without limit. Vegetables and fruits should be chopped into tiny pieces and offered as a mixed salad. Wild plants that are favored include dandelion, chickweed, coltsfoot, cress, plantain, groundsel, clover, and shepherd's purse to name but a few. Make a point of finding out which plants are a feature of your locality and which are known to be poisonous. If in doubt, leave them out.

### SOFTFOODS

The singular advantage of supplying your stock

Lavender Finches are mainly an insectivorous species. They should always be supplied with a reasonable amount of both natural and artificial insectivorous food as well as a mixture of canary and millet seed.

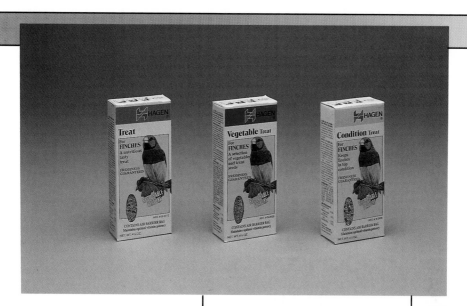

with commercial softfood mixes is that they are both convenient and rich in proteins. They save one from the task of cultivating or gathering earthworms, insects, and their like. Further, they carry no risk of being carriers of disease. You can always purchase various worms and maggots for feeding to your breeding birds, or to non breeders as a treat. All food of this type should be washed.

## SUPPLEMENTS

Numerous bird tonics and vitamin supplements are produced to improve the health or feather of your birds if supplied. Basically, if your stock takes a wide ranging diet of seed, greenfoods, and softfoods, looks healthy, and is breeding well, any supplements given cannot help anymore. A missing vitamin is unlikely in a varied diet. Color enhancing foods may appeal to you for those species that have red in their plumage. Color often deteriorates in stock due to a lack of livefoods, or a certain group of plants may not be available. Be aware that color enhancers are only temporary and need to be supplied prior to each molt. Generally, their use has little benefit to the true birdkeeper because it distorts reality. Feeding your finches is not an exact science. If common sense and a variety of foods are applied, you will not go wrong. Always be prepared to listen to the advice of experienced keepers, but never assume that all you are told is the only truth. The latter you will observe in the health and vigor, or lack of it, of your stock.

"Treats" serve various purposes: vitamin and mineral supplementation, conditioning for breeding, dietary balancing, and the like. The treats pictured here are from Rolf C. Hagen Corp.

# Breeding

Any birdkeeper that has kept a number of finches for a short period of time invariably becomes overwhelmed with a desire to breed birds. It is a fascinating and deeply rewarding part of aviculture, but also one that should not be undertaken lightly. First, be sure space for the future offspring, and cash for the provisions needed, is available. Experience can be gained with an easily bred species such as the Zebra Finch. Once confident in your ability as a breeder, move on to a species that even though not costly to purchase, represent much more of a challenge in its breeding needs. Some birds breed with little or no prompting, others are very particular in regard to the nesting site, box, materials, and general environmental conditions. Others, such as the gorgeously colored Gouldian Finches, are notorious for not rearing their young. In this case, the services of a foster species may be required. Given the potential needs of the many species from which to choose your initial stock, this chapter can do no more than provide a skeleton of basic information. Seek books that are more specific to the particular birds you plan to keep, or a book specific to the breeding of finches. Attention regarding feeding needs and nest materials is especially important to all breeding birds.

**BREEDING SEASON**

The breeding season commences, for the majority of birdkeepers, in

Creme-White Shafttail. The mutations of the Shafttail Finch have a unique beauty all their own. These Creme-White Shafttails show how a bird of somber and quiet colors can achieve an ultimate beauty.

Green Singing Finch. Green Singing Finches are ideal companions for waxbills because they are better breeders than the average waxbill and often act as "tutors" for these little birds.

the spring and terminates during the late summer or early autumn. At these times the number of daylight hours are at a peak and greenfoods are plentiful. With artificial light and background heat, many birds can be induced to breed year 'round. The fact that this is possible should not prompt you to breed your stock in excess. This merely reduces the vigor of the hens, who will in turn have a shorter breeding life. The offspring also tend to become progressively weaker with subsequent clutches; hens therefore require a period of time to recover after each couple of nests.

**BREEDING CONDITION**
It is crucial that only really fit birds are bred. Hens that are overweight or

The Blue Capped Cordon Bleu. This finch adequately fulfills the many reasons for its high ranking popularity. It is one of the few finches with a beautiful shade of sky blue. Its shape is gracefully simple, and it has a peaceful nature.

in poor condition may become eggbound. If planning to cage breed finches they will be better off if allowed to spend a period beforehand in an outdoor aviary, or at least in a large indoor flight. This permits them to exercise and develop good muscle tone. As a general guide, the best age to commence breeding is the following Spring of the year they were hatched. This makes them at least eight months old. They could be bred at a younger age, however, it is not advised if health and vigor are to be priorities.

**COMPATIBILITY**

Just because a pair of birds comprises one of each sex by no means ensures they will breed. They must be compatible. To increase the chances that this will be so, pairs or groups should be placed together well ahead of the planned breeding season. In this manner the birds can be observed to see who gets along well with each other. The final inducement to mate comes once a nestbox is placed into the cage or aviary. If a pair shows no interest in mating several reasons may be the cause:

1. The pair just does not like each other!
2. The nestbox is not to the pair's liking.
3. The nestbox site does not appeal to the pair.
4. The pair is being subjected to too many disturbances (noises, children, dogs, car headlights at night, and so on).
5. One or both of the pair is not in hard breeding condition.

The problem itself will suggest what remedial action should be taken. Of course, initially the problem may not be easy to identify, such as nest site or box. Provision of numerous styles of nestboxes in various locations (low, high, well screened, and so forth) will help in determining the conditions your particular birds want. If the birds are cage paired and refuse to go to nest, even though conditions seem ideal, either place them apart, yet visible to each other, or provide alternative mates for them.

**NESTBOXES**

A range of nestboxes exist that finches may choose to use. Most prefer the covered type nests of wicker, but wooden nestboxes are also used. Both feature a small hole towards the top. With experience you will no doubt start to experiment and make your own nestboxes. More

Diamond Fire Tail Finch. The diet of the Fire Tail consists of standard seed and insectivorous mixes available from your local pet store. Livefoods are also recommended.

White Java Rice Bird. The White Java Rice Bird is a mutation which occurred in captivity. It is not an albino.

nestboxes should always be made available than pairs of birds. In colony or mixed aviaries, site nests at comparable locations and heights to reduce the risk of squabbling. Some species will of course prefer secluded locations in bushes, others, such as those that are very well established, may not be at all concerned whether or not the site offers privacy.

Some species roost in their nestboxes after the breeding season, therefore, the boxes should be left in place year 'round. Others do not, and the boxes can be removed when the season is over.

## NESTING MATERIALS

Finches, collectively, utilize a wide range of nesting materials. It is a case of supplying those known to be favored by the species you keep. Most are happy with dried grasses or small bird feathers. Commercial nesting material, dried moss, and even dried leaves are used by some species. Certain species, such as weavers, need strands of raffia to weave very intricate hanging nests. Ample nesting material should be supplied so the finches are not discouraged from preparing a suitable nest. One learns just how much material a pair needs through trial and error.

## INCUBATION

The incubation period varies among species. During very dry summers lightly spray the nest box daily with water to help maintain a reasonable level of humidity. Nestboxes placed in the flight should

St. Helena Waxbills are very active and quite hardy when kept under the proper conditions. Pairs are best bred if they have the enclosure to themselves.

be of a more solid construction than those sited in the shelter. Wooden boxes are best with hinged lids so that they can be inspected to see that all is going well. If possible, these boxes should also be made so they can be dismantled for thorough cleaning at the end of the season.

**BASIC BREEDING INFORMATION**

Finches lay an average of 2-6 eggs. Larger clutches are, of course, possible. The eggs are incubated by both parents in most species. In some species the role of the male is merely to sit for short periods while the hen is away from the nest. Actual "sitting" to incubate the eggs may not start until after the second egg, or until the last egg, is laid.

The incubation period ranges from 12-15 days and the chicks leave the nest between 13-23 days old. By the time the chicks are 30 days old they should be feeding by themselves. Some may do so before this time, others after. The temperature condition in which the chicks live is a major factor in how quickly they develop.

**NEST INSPECTION**

Inspecting a nest to check on the progress of the chicks is very much a subjective matter and is also influenced by the species involved. Zebra Finches, for example, are so domesticated that they rarely resent intrusion. Conversely, a rarely bred species may desert its nest if it is constantly interfered with from inspections. With a rare species, a breeder

Red Headed Finch. Red Headed Finches are more frequently seen now than in the past. A cousin to the Cutthroat Finch, it is slightly larger and more dominant than the Cutthroat.

may remove one or more eggs and foster them under a different species simply to increase the chance that at least one or two of the chicks will survive. Nest inspection allows for the removal of dead chicks as well as a tidying up of the nest (if the parents are not attending to this chore). If the hen has a very large clutch it is advised to foster some of the eggs to a hen with a small one. Most breeders of popular finches, as a general guide, try to keep any eye on development, but do so while the hens are away from their nests. This is easily achieved with cage bred birds which have external nestboxes fitted, and is more difficult with birds that are breeding within a screen of shrub branches.

## BREEDING PROBLEMS

There are, of course, many things that can go wrong during the breeding period. Discussion of one or two major problems, as well as some causal factors should be mentioned.

Eggbinding: This is a condition in which a hen is unable to expel an egg. It may happen for a number of reasons such as a softshelled egg, in which the hen's contractions fail to move it along the

oviduct, an especially large egg, or the hen may be overweight and sufficient muscular pressure on the egg is not exerted. In any case, the hen strains so hard that all of her energy is used, and eventually she collapses on the floor in a very distressed state. Unless the hen is attended to quickly, she will probably die. Transfer her immediately to a hospital cage, the heat alone may enable the egg to be passed. The desired temperature should be about 90° F (32° C). Carefully smearing olive oil around her vent may also help. You might also be able to maneuver the egg along the oviduct and out, but this is risky because the egg could rupture

Star Finch. The Star Finch is a very cheerful singer. Its song consists of a pretty warble that is not uttered very frequently. It is a more varied and quicker type of song than the Green Singing Finch.

within causing peritonitis. A vet may suggest a helpful injection, but unfortunately the shock of this to such a distressed small hen could prove fatal. All in all, if heat fails the prognosis is not good. This strongly suggests preventative husbandry as, by far, the desired state. Do not attempt to breed too early in the season when there could be late frosts or cold, damp weather. Be sure that the females are extremely fit. Ensure that sufficient calcium is available, as well as a varied diet, to protect against avitaminosis (lack of vitamins). Do not be greedy in trying to beat records for how many clutches you can derive from a hen. Three is recommended, four at most—beyond this trouble with your female will come sooner or later.

Nest Desertion: If you interfere with a nest too often, or if something frightens the parents during the night, the nest may be deserted. Other things such as mite or lice infestation cause great discomfort, such that the female only wants to leave the nest. A treatment with a cat flea powder may cure the nest and the bird, or a total disinfection may be required.

Temperature Extremes: Excessive heat or cold obviously affect the development of eggs and should be safeguarded against.

Damaged Eggs: Eggs can be damaged as they are rolled by the hen, or scratched from the claws of the parents. Bacteria can gain access to the egg which will then become addled. If a crack is spotted early, try and cover it with nail varnish. It should hatch as normal as long as bacteria did not already penetrate it. To prevent this, carefully trim the tips of the birds nails with canine nail clippers before setting them up to nest.

Hens have also been known to cannibalize their eggs. The problem can have a genetic base, reflect a lack of a needed nutrient, or indicate a concern of the environment she is in. Before deciding she is not a worthwhile member of breeding stock try to discover what the problem may be. Bear in mind that if the problem is genetic she could have inherited this trait from her father, not necessarily from her mother. This complicates tracking backwards. Detailed record keeping is therefore a must for any serious breeder.

**Opposite page:** Pintailed Whydah. When in full color, the male Pintail is very vicious and spiteful in the aviary. It should not be housed with any but the rather large species of finch.

**CHICK REARING**

After the chicks fledge (leave the nest) they will continue to be fed by the male and any older siblings that might still be in the aviary. At this time the female is preoccupied with laying her second clutch of eggs. Once the chicks are feeding on enough seed by themselves they can be moved into a nursery cage. This should contain low perches as well as food in dishes scattered on the floor. Continue feeding softfood to them. Once you are fully satisfied they are eating enough to sustain their body weight, they can be sold. If they are cage bred and you plan to place them in an aviary the weather must be warm. The fledgling period is a very difficult time for young chicks and many losses can be encountered from any lack of care, food, temperature control, or hygiene at this time. Likewise, when experiencing their first molt they are easily stressed. This places them at a greater than normal risk to illness. They enter their first molt at about eight weeks of age and complete it by the time they are approximately three months old.

**LEG BANDS**

Leg bands come in two forms, closed metal bands used as permanent forms of identification, and split bands for temporary identification. Closed bands are fitted when the chicks are a few days old and usually the breeder's name, code, or year the bird hatched are inscribed. Split

African Fire Finch. Fire Finches are among the most calm of all finches. They rarely panic. They are gregarious, happy, and peaceful but will become aggressive if need be to protect their nests.

Blue Capped Cordon Bleu. The male of this species has his entire head and neck blue instead of brown on top of its head and nape. The females of all Cordon Bleu species are very difficult to distinguish from each other. A female Blue Capped will sometimes have blue on the forehead.

bands can be fitted at any age. Some finch societies require closed bands be fitted to any exhibition stock, while others do not. Some breeders are quite happy to fit closed bands, others will not on two accounts. First, the bands must be fitted while the chicks are only days old and some breeders will not disturb the nests at this time. Secondly, bands can create problems such as becoming clogged with fecal matter, or chicks, and later the adults they grow into, becoming caught on netting or shrubs. The subject is therefore one in which you must decide for yourself. In species where there are no obligatory society or government regulations, it is usually mandatory to fit closed bands on any birds that are indigenous to your country, proving they were legally bred under captive conditions. Such birds must carry a band if they are sold. In the event that fecal matter should compress between the ring and a chick's leg it can be carefully removed by being soaked a little at a time. Never try to force dry matter away from the leg. Should a banded bird suffer a leg injury this could swell and create problems. In such a case take the bird to your vet who will use a special tool to cut the band. Failure to do so might result in restricted blood flow to the toes.

# Exhibition

The foreign bird show is the shop window for the entire hobby of aviculture. At such an exhibition hobbyists have the opportunity to see more finch-like birds than at any other single venue. A vast array of species, and all the color forms they may be available in are for spectators viewing. This gives one a yardstick by which to judge the birds that may later be purchased. Breeders and exhibitors compare their stock to that of other breeders in a competitive framework. It establishes them as breeders of repute. This has the benefit that it is much easier to sell surplus stock, and probably get a better price for it too. At the larger shows there are trade stands that sell all of the

Parson Finch. The Parson Finch is very much like the Shafttail except for the following characteristics: Black beak instead of orange; square, short tail instead of long, tapering tail; and a pale brown chest instead of a soft pale gray.

specialist appliances, seed, and indeed birds. Exhibitions are also important social occasions where new friends that share in the love of birdkeeping can be met.

**SIZE AND TYPES OF SHOW**

A bird exhibition ranges in size from small, restricted to members, to enormous, spread over a number of days and attracting hobbyists from all over the world. Some shows are restricted to single highly popular species, such as Zebra Finches. For most finch enthusiasts the open foreign bird show holds the most interest. At this sort of exhibition all the birds seen in aviculture, parrot-like, finch-like, and softbilled birds are on display. The large national exhibitions include all of the groups just mentioned, birds that are indigenous to your country, and those which can be legally kept if wearing a closed ring. Many of these birds are finch-like. Shows are advertised well in advance in the cage and aviary magazines of your country and by major bird clubs, and societies.

**SHOW CAGES**

In order to exhibit your finch-like birds, a cage appropriate to the species

Owl Finch. Owl Finches have a very pleasing appearance and a friendly and delightful personality as well as a peaceful congeniality to all other birds.

Black Bellied Fire Finch. Fire Finches are probably the best breeders in the waxbill family. Livefood is required during the nesting season. In planted aviaries these birds prove to do very well because they can gather a great deal of livefood from the plants.

you keep is required. In some species there may be no fixed styles, but the cage must be of the foreign finch type. This means it is to be painted black outside, with a white or pastel shade inside. It can carry no form of identification on it other than a number given for that show known only to the officials. This way the judge has no idea who owns the bird being assessed. Show cages are available from specialist suppliers, and local clubs.

**YOUR LOCAL BIRD SOCIETY**

It is recommended that one joins a local foreign bird club. The benefits are considerable regardless of whether or not a choice is made to become an exhibitor. In the latter case, you are given much advice and instruction on how to prepare and exhibit birds. Advice is also gained on cages, aviaries, and general husbandry techniques. Further, there will be members with birds for sale, and of course they are also potential customers for your stock. They will be useful contacts for people they know who want birds, but which they are not able to supply. As with many things in life it is not just

European Goldfinch. The European Goldfinch is pretty, hardy, a fine songster, and a reasonably good breeder. It is one of the most popular cage birds in Europe and is well known to American Fanciers.

Society Finch. Unfortunately, the sexes of these birds are alike. The males can only be determined when they are seen displaying to the hens. This they do with an amusing bowing motion while uttering their harsh, squeaky little song.

what you know, but who you know, so do support your local and national foreign bird societies.

### SHOW JUDGING

Exhibition birds are entered into various classes based on their species, previous show record (whether they have won first place awards), sex, and color markings (in those species where appropriate). There are many potential show classes such as, Australian Finches or Current Year Bred Birds. Those first noted are the basic classes that are scheduled at all shows. In some species a written standard of excellence gives points for various bodily parts, condition, and color markings. Others are judged for their over all plumage and condition.

The winning birds go forward to compete with other class winners of their type (cocks, hens, colors, and so on). By this process of elimination there is a best cock and hen of each species or group. These eventually compete for the Best in Show Award which is normally decided by a panel of judges. In some countries the judging is done behind closed doors, and in others the exhibitors and the public are able to watch. Unlike the systems used in dogs, cats, and rabbits, where the exhibit gains status, in birds, it is the exhibitor that is graded based on success. A breeder thus becomes a champion breeder. Hereafter, he or she can only exhibit in classes with comparable breeders.

## PREPARING THE SHOW FINCH

To become a consistently successful exhibitor entails a tremendous amount of work and dedication. Clearly, birds must be very good examples of their species. But more, they must be maintained in immaculate plumage and good general health. They must also be trained to show themselves to their best advantage when being assessed by a judge under conditions that are far removed from those in their aviary or cage. The potential show bird begins its career soon after it goes through its first molt. The breeder picks out potential youngsters to add to the existing team from previous years. The young birds are steadily trained to become familiar with the show cage. This is done by placing the show cage door to the door of the stock cage. Tidbits are placed in the show cage and the bird is quite happy to enter for these treats. Soon it becomes quite happy in the show cage, and remains there for progressively longer periods of time without showing any signs of nervousness. The show cage is then sited in various locations of the birdroom and exhibitor's home. In this way, the exhibit becomes familiar with different surroundings and different people peering in at it. If this training is done at a high standard the result is a bird that hops from perch to perch totally unconcerned with what is happening outside of its cage during a show. The judge is then able to assess its merits without problem. An inadequately trained bird flutters to the floor and attempts to "hide" in a corner when people get near its cage. Such a bird cannot be assessed, and therefore, has no chance of a win or placing. The

Zebra Finch. This is the best known of all Australian Finches. Zebra Finches are perky, hardy, pompous little birds with a ridiculous song sounding like the piping of a toy whistle. They are fond of greenfood. Heads of small meadow grass should always be supplied.

Colored much like the White Headed Nun is the Pale Headed Munia. A number of nun forms having whitish heads may be distinguished, and which of them deserve specific status remains controversial.

plumage of the show bird must be immaculate. Show birds are taken from aviary or stock cage situations and housed by themselves as the show season approaches. Special mist spray conditioners are available for show birds. You can alternatively use a mild solution of water and glycerin to give an added sheen to the feathers.

## THE SHOW—BREED COMPROMISE

Many breeders will not exhibit their birds either because of the considerable amount of work and costs involved, or because of the fact that showing and

breeding, while being obviously a natural combination in one sense, are not in another. The show season is during the non breeding time of the year, autumn through spring. It is a very short period, in real terms, in which to bring a breeding bird into show condition, or more importantly, the reverse. If a bird enjoys a successful show season it most certainly takes a toll on its energy. The stress of transportation, long hours in the show cage, and constant life in a small cage, are not conducive for bringing a bird into hard breeding condition. As a

result it is hardly fair to expect such a bird to settle down and rear two or three rounds of chicks after such a season. Exhibitors overcome this situation by only showing their birds one or two seasons and then "retiring" the birds to become breeding stock. Some exhibitors also have a large show team which enables them to not to be constantly exhibiting the same birds, thus tasking their energy. A large team, however, is costly to upkeep and train, and although it offers many rewards, is not without a price, which must be carefully considered in advance. Because of this, many exhibitors are only what might be termed "casual". They show at local exhibitions where the competition is not so fierce, and the demands on the exhibitor/breeder are less costly in hard currency (travel, entry fees) and time.

There is little doubt that without the exhibition side of aviculture, the hobby would be many years behind the state it has reached at this time. Regardless of whether or not one plans to show birds, it is found that just being a regular show visitor is both fascinating and addicting! It keeps one in touch with the entire hobby. Do be sure to visit some bird shows before any sort of commitment is made to cages, aviaries, or birds themselves. You will be very glad you did.

Owl Finch. Owl Finches prefer open nests to enclosed boxes in most cases. The parents are inclined to be a little too peaceful though they are nevertheless devoted to the task of rearing their offspring.

# Health Care

Preventative medicine husbandry is nowhere so important as it is with finches. Their small size, coupled with their very rapid metabolic rates, means they are not only difficult to treat once ill, but that they can die within a matter of hours of first being diagnosed as unwell. Matters are made more difficult because birds seem to be able to mask illness until it reaches an advanced stage. The fact that their bodies are covered with feathers also

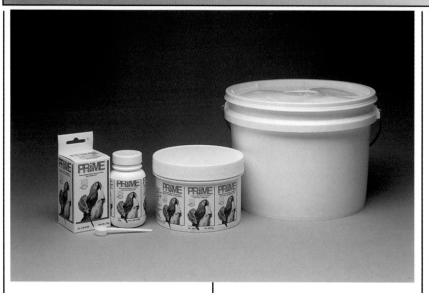

makes things more difficult for the owner. You cannot easily see if a bird is underweight as you can with a dog, cat, or rabbit, nor can the skin be easily examined. Finally, the shock of intra muscular injections, or even the stress of being examined by your vet, can itself kill the bird. Accepting this latter situation as a reality does not mean veterinary treatment should not be attempted. Inaccurate home diagnosis and poor treatment are far worse than the risks mentioned here. The advantage of a veterinary examination, even if a bird does die, is that it can pinpoint the causal problem, whereby the rest of your stock may be safeguarded. In an age when finches are becoming costly, this is an important

consideration when pondering vet fees versus the value of the bird. Given the fact that most avian diseases can only be correctly diagnosed by blood samples and microscopy of fecal matter, feathers, or skin tissue, failure to seek veterinary advice would be classed as very poor management where aviary and breeding stock are concerned.

## QUARANTINE & HOSPITAL CAGES

Once your collection consists of a few finches, it is imperative to quarantine all stock subsequently added. To effect this, one or more cages sited as far from your main stock as possible should be obtained. Further, at yet another site, should be a hospital cage. These two

are acclimatized, routinely treated for worms, and carefully observed to see they are eating adequate amounts and types of food. A period of 21 days is sufficient for most diseases to manifest themselves if they are present. This period also allows the newcomers to adjust to any localized bacteria they may never have before encountered in their previous home.

cage types require isolation from your main stock to reduce the risk of direct, or proximinal, spread of pathogens. Surprisingly, many aviary owners do not feature these facilities as separate units. As a result, the risk of disease, should it arise, could reach epidemic levels.

Quarantine cages should be as large as you can allow space for. They should be thoroughly disinfected before and after each use. Ornate furnishings are not required, only dowel perches and food/water dishes. During the quarantine period the birds

After they have passed through quarantine they should be placed into a stock cage in the main birdroom for a further 7-14 days. This allows for the familiarization to local pathogens to be completed in the absence of direct contact with your stock.

Many birdkeepers might disagree with this seemingly long period of introduction, but the hard reality is that when a small finch moves from one home to another it is exposed to many pathogens, and is stressed as well. The more gradual you can make its change to your home the easier this will be, and the greater the time for problems to be seen or overcome by the bird's natural immune system.

Always keep a record of the source of every one of your birds. This may be of value at a later date. Inquire about the diet your newly acquired birds were receiving, and whether they were acclimatized to outdoor aviaries or not. Very often, novice aviary owners purchase birds from pet shops or birdfarms where birds have been kept in heated quarters. They then release the birds into an aviary

Lady Gouldian Finch & Cutthroat. Lady Gouldians and Cutthroats are not good cage birds. Both require much room, such as in an aviary, to maintain good feather condition.

where they quickly catch chill, depending on the weather at the time. Acclimatization should be carefully conducted over a period of weeks.

The hospital cage can be a regular stock cage. See that it is well coated with a washable, non-toxic paint. It should contain one or two low perches, a thermometer, food/water dishes, and a larger shallow dish of water protected by mesh (so the bird cannot fall into it) to ensure sufficient humidity in the cage.

Purchase an infrared lamp, together with a cage clamp. Ideally, the lamp should be wired through a thermostat in, or close to, the cage to ensure a constant, non fluctuating, temperature. Place the lamp at one end of the outside of the cage so that the finch can move to a slightly cooler and more comfortable position if it feels stressed from excess heat. If this is noted, reduce the temperature by two degrees. The suggested temperature in a hospital cage is at least 90°F (32°C). Heat alone is amazingly successful in

Tri-Colored Nun. Nuns rarely rear young in captivity and determining the sex of the birds is very difficult. Behavior is a sure sign. The male sings poorly and dances comically to the hen.

Cordon Bleu Finch. Although this bird is delicate and susceptible to illness from sudden changes in temperature, once it is acclimatized it can live for quite a few years.

taking a bird from being apparently at death's door to a complete recovery.

A makeshift hospital cage can be fashioned by covering a stock cage with clear plastic, but leaving the door exposed for ventilation. The cage can then be placed on a heater pad or even a hot water bottle, and the temperature will rise. A 40 or 60 watt bulb placed near the front of the cage is an alternative to this, but should be shaded so the patient does not have to endure the glare of the light. It will otherwise become stressed, which is counter productive to your objective.

## HYGIENE

Higher standards of hygiene lower the risk that pathogens will colonize in your birdroom or aviaries. The following are those areas that you should be especially meticulous about because they can so easily be "put off" until another day.They take on a greater importance when the summer months arrive because higher temperatures are more conducive to bacterial reproduction than the colder months. You should therefore double up on cleaning routines during very hot and humid weather.

1. Keep perches very clean—Wash perches each week to keep them free of fecal matter and hardened food. Birds often wipe their beaks on perches and bacteria is easily passed from one bird to another. The same is true of cage bars. Always ensure that birds are not forced to sit closely together on perches. Crowded perches increase the chances of direct transmission of parasites and bacteria.
2. Clean food and water cups at least once each week and preferably more often. Replace any

that are cracked or chipped.Clean all cages each week, and do not forget to repaint them each year. It is wise to have a few spare cages to rotate stock. In this way you can disinfect and leave empty for a short period of time.

3. Thoroughly clean all nestboxes before and after they are used. Replace those that start to look scratched, chipped, and generally worn.

4. Hose down flights each week. If there are earth areas in your aviaries, periodically blow torch them to kill the eggs of parasitic worms. It is best to concrete flights.

5. Wear disposable surgical gloves when handling sick birds, and wash your hands with a germicidal soap after attending cleaning chores in the birdroom.

6. Wear a nylon overall when working with your birds. This minimizes parasitic transportation on your clothes.

7. Your stockroom should not be "open house" to just any bird breeder. They may have sick birds and can transport pathogens to your birdroom on their clothes, shoes, or person. Know who you invite into the birdroom.

8. Remove, or dispose of, all debris taken from the cages. Do not leave it in piles or trash cans anywhere near your birds.

## OVERCROWDING

We are all tempted to keep more birds than

Crested Society Finch. Mutations among Society Finches are also available such as this Crested Society. There are some breeders who find that their best crested birds are derived from one crested parent and one non-crested.

perhaps is prudent (from a husbandry viewpoint). Be aware of this weakness. Exactly what constitutes overcrowding is impossible to be specific about because many factors must be considered. For example, the amount of sunlight, the extent of ventilation, and the size and quality of the caging all affect how healthy a given volume of air is. The fitting of ionizers and a means of temperature control will, with the other considerations, allow a higher stocking density than if these are substandard features of the birdroom.

Even so, there is a limit to how many birds you should keep under one roof. If your collection numbers in excess of a hundred, rather than a few dozen birds, it is suggested that the erection of a second birdroom would make a great deal of sense.

**STRESS**

Stress is without doubt the most important precursor of avian conditions and diseases. It greatly reduces the effectiveness of a bird's natural immune defenses because it uses up valuable nervous energy. The situations that create stress include the following: transportation, overcrowding, poor nutrition, lack of exercise, aggressive birds, excessive interference by the owner, handling of birds, and poor temperature conditions. Many of the stress situations are themselves

ideal conditions for pathogenic multiplication creating a double negative. Not surprisingly, a small bird quickly deteriorates under these conditions. Further, given that the conditions are not ideal, and birds are able to mask problems, the rapid spread of disease is often a forgone conclusion once it strikes a stockroom that has management problems.

## WHEN TROUBLE ARRIVES

The vast majority of conditions and diseases arise in aviaries due to some management inadequacy. If steps have been taken to ensure your stock's well being, the problems you encounter should be minimal. However, the fact that pathogens are always in the air means even the best run set-up can find itself

Violet Eared Waxbills cannot successfully withstand excessive dampness or rapid drops in temperature. They are best kept indoors at temperatures higher than 50°F.

Java Rice Bird. The overall size of the Java Rice Bird is a heavy bodied 5½ inches including the tail. The tail itself is just over an inch. Since Rice Birds are large, they should be housed with larger finches.

suffering from a problem of one sort or another. An ill bird may pass through your screening process because the disease may lay dormant for months, or your neighbor's birds may be less than well cared for and they can be a constant source of airborne disease in your locality. The minute you feel that a bird is acting, or looking less than it should, isolate it. If it is one of a pair it would be wise to let its partner remain with it. This reduces stress, and if the bird proves to be ill the

chances are that its partner also contracted the problem. It should be documented when the bird was isolated and why.

This is the beginning of the case history which is later important to diagnose both the problem and the cause. Slightly increase the temperature in the isolation cage. If the condition is only minor, this may arrest further problems. If the birds display watery fecal matter, stop feeding greenfoods for 24 hours and see what happens. If possible, where

Diamond Fire Tail Finch. A heavyweight among finches, in captivity it is steady to the point of lethargy in many instances. Obesity can be a problem, and during breeding season, if it is housed with other birds, it may throw its weight around.

single and paired birds are caged, inspect their regular cage and see what foods have been eaten, not just what has been supplied.

At this time note in the case history the following information which a vet will no doubt want to know if the illness progresses and veterinary advice is sought.

1. Length of time you have owned the bird.
2. Place where the bird was obtained.
3. Details of the diet.
4. Any recent illness the bird or other birds it has been in contact with has had.
5. Potential pathogenic sources such as piles of rotting vegetation near your aviaries.
6. Number of birds that occupy the same birdroom/aviary complex.
7. Rate the clinical signs have progressed.

You should of course carefully check all other birds to see if any are displaying similar signs. If many of them are, or do so within a short period of time, you will not be able to isolate them all and therefore treatment will have to be handled as a whole.

Should this ever be the case, your aviaries require to become "out of bounds" to all people other than those of your family. It

Star Finches are generally regarded as hardy birds. They thrive on direct sunlight and should be provided with heat during the winter.

would also be wise to cancel any show plans pending the problem be totally corrected. This is only fair to the other exhibitors.

Once the potential patients have been isolated, thoroughly clean their former cage and everything in it, perches, accessories, dishes, nests, etc.

## DIAGNOSIS

Diagnosis of other than the most obvious problems, such as mite or lice

invasion, is best left to your veterinarian. Many of the clinical signs of disease are similar. A wrong diagnosis can make matters worse, not better.

The duration of a given medicine is a matter of critical importance because many drugs are not pathogen specific. This means they will also kill beneficial bacteria. If they fail to achieve their objective within a short period of time, continued administration can be

dangerous to such small birds. Bear in mind when relating clinical signs to your vet that the bird's heart beat and respiratory rate will increase from being transferred to an isolation cage. Take special notice of this before you make the transfer. Usually a vet will need to examine the bird. When transporting the bird to the vet, be sure its cage is covered with a blanket or similar if the weather is cool to cold. This way it will not be at any greater risk of catching a chill than if it was in your aviary.

## TREATMENTS

In recent years there has been a considerable improvement in drugs and other treatments available to pet birds. Veterinarians are generally far more knowledgeable on avian problems than in the past. It must be said that finch-like birds are still not as readily treated as the psittacines, due to their small size. In spite of the increased knowledge, there is a vast number of unknown data in respect to cage and aviary bird diseases.

Birds can be given medication via their food and water. Oral administration directly to the crop, or simply into the beak, is only an option if the bird is too weak to eat or drink. Intra muscular injections are also possible, but should only be administered by a veterinarian. Some birds literally drop dead within minutes of being handled, others are able to withstand the trauma. Treatment for external parasites must include all of the caging as well as the bird. Repeat treatments are necessary 7-10 days later in order to eradicate the eggs that hatch, and those which were not affected by the first treatment. Repeat

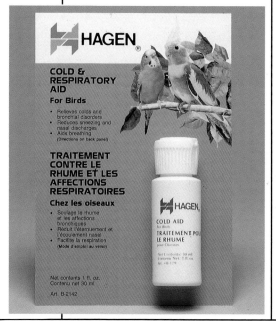

Commercial products such as this Rolf C. Hagen respiratory aid can help to keep finches healthy.

treatments are usually required when treating internal parasitic worms. Often these parasites are introduced to your aviary via earthworms, slugs, and ground insects, as well as from the droppings of wild birds. Certain pathogens, such as E. coli, also infect other animals such as farm or pet pigs. The source of a disease, therefore, may not necessarily be from other birds. Once a bird has been treated with drugs or heat it should be carefully acclimatized back to its normal cage or aviary

Peter's Twinspot. In the wild, this magnificent finch frequents dense brush and thorn tangles on river banks, and spends most of its time on the ground among the undergrowth.

temperature over a number of days by steady reduction of the temperature. If you have treated a hen for eggbinding do not return her to a breeding situation until the following season. Do not return recently recovered birds to an aviary if the weather is turning cold. Be sure you have taken the needed steps to eliminate, or at least minimize, the risk of the disease happening again.

## ACCIDENTS

Should a bird ever cut itself on a sharp wire end, or similar protrusion, the wound must be bathed with a mild saline solution or a germicidal soap, and then covered with an antiseptic ointment or liquid. A coagulant is a good idea to keep in your first aid kit and this could be applied. Minor wounds clear up within a day or two but it is wise to isolate the bird so you can check that the cut is healing correctly. Broken wings and legs are difficult to treat: the suggested treatment is to place the bird in an isolation cage with very low perches. The limb will mend, but not always in the normal position. Other than this the bird, assuming it recovers its ordeal, can live a normal life.

The knowledge of preventative husbandry is all together better than one of disease recognition and treatment because it avoids the latter being needed.

**Opposite page:** Cutthroat Finch. The bright red slash across the throat of the male gives this bird its name. It is quite aggressive during breeding season and should remain undisturbed.

# Popular Species

The taxonomic groups we are regarding as finch-like for the purposes of this book consist of three families, Fringilidae, Estrildidae, and Ploceidae of which there are about 408 species. Very few of these can be regarded as being popular in aviculture, and a number of others are available to a greater or lesser degree, depending on the country you live in and the time of year. The species mentioned in this chapter are generally available to birdkeepers in Britain, Europe, the USA and Canada, but supplies are rather limited to unavailable in Australia.

The true finches of the family Fringillidae number about 121 species, but they contribute only a relatively small number of avicultural favorites. The most popular "finches" are members of the family Estrildidae, of which there are 131 species. The weaver and whydah birds, family Ploceidae, which include the many common sparrows of the world, number 156 species. Only a relatively small number are popular in aviculture because they are rather more difficult to breed and to cater for. There is a need for birdkeepers to make concerted efforts to establish some of the more readily available species that are presently "consumed" from the wild as breeding birds. It should never be assumed that because a species numbers in its millions in its native country its availability is thus assured, and at a low price. The Australian ban on the export and import of all animal forms in 1959 underlined only too

Aurora Finch. In a suitable aviary most pairs will start nesting as soon as they have had time to settle down. Results are often erratic. Aurora Finches will not rear their young without livefood, but mealworms should be rationed.

Star Finch. The Star Finch is one of the best aviary birds.

emphatically that supplies can dry up almost overnight. Since that event, more and more countries have steadily restricted the number of birds they allow to be exported, some even imposed complete bans. What today might be an inexpensive and common import could tomorrow be an avian rarity if breeding stocks are not established. The need for livefood during the early lives of the chicks of many species is vital to their survival and is important to consider when establishing breeding stocks. If it is not provided, the chicks fail to gain the needed nutrients, and the strong possibility that the parents will either desert them or throw them from the nest exists.

### FAMILY FRINGILLIDAE

**Canary** *Serinus canaria* **13cm(5in)**
Without a doubt, the most well known member of this family is the ever popular canary in its many varieties. Although not

regarded as being a "foreign" or exotic finch, any novice would be advised to include a variety, such as the Border or Gloster, in a collection. Their brilliant plumage coupled with the sweet song of the male birds, makes them a desirable aviary or pet bird. Canaries prefer an open nestpan for breeding purposes that is lined with a special felt. The sexes are similar and can only be distinguished during breeding periods.

**Green Singing Finch *Serinus mozambicus* 12cm (4.7in)**
   This little African finch is also known as the Yellow Fronted Canary because of its yellow chest and under parts. It sports yellow bars over its eyes, and the remaining plumage is basically brown. The hen is a less brilliant version of the male which is noted for its very pleasant song. This is a readily available bird at a modest price. It is hardy and long lived, with a number of birds documented to live 15-20 years. It is a willing if not prolific breeder that prefers a canary nest pan. Its singular drawback is that it is a little aggressive in a mixed aviary. It is not so much a dangerous bird as one that creates

Assembled Seed Dispenser. Seed dispensers of this type are often used in finch aviaries. It is a good idea to check this device often to be sure that it has not jammed.

Green Singing Finch. The Green Singing Finch only joins with a mate during breeding season, then they separate. The courtship is inclined to be rather aggressive and usually results in the hen getting some of her feathers pulled out by the male.

disturbance by its intrusive nature. A close and equally readily available relative is the Gray Singing Finch, *S.leucopygious*. This is a slightly smaller bird, also known as the White Rumped Canary or Seedeater. The sexes are similar. Its plumage is basically gray being lighter on the chest and under parts. Also a fine singer, it is perhaps slightly less hardy than the previous species.

**Goldfinch** *Carduelis carduelis* **13cm (5in)**
This gorgeously colored bird must be close banded to be offered for sale in Britain and the USA. Its main colors consist of a red head with a black bar from beak to eye, white behind the red, then a black band. The body is a soft brown and the wings are tipped with black and yellow. Sexes are similar. In breeding, Goldfinches prefer a well planted

aviary: wild plants are greatly favored as well as insectivorous commercial diets. A specialist breeder is usually the main source of supply. A relative of this species is the Greenfinch, *Chloris chloris*. It is more soberly colored in a dull green and brown with just a flash of yellow in the wing feathers. Sexes again are similar. It is larger than the Goldfinch and should be kept with birds of similar size otherwise it will prove to be rather a bully and disruptive to smaller finches.

## Other Fringilids

Of the numerous other Fringilid species only the Bullfinches, Grosbeaks, and Rosefinchs could be said to be reasonably popular in aviculture. For the average first time birdkeeper these birds have the disadvantage of being rather large, 14-25 cm (5.5-10 in), in length. They are therefore not recommended for inclusion within a mixed aviary containing smaller finches. As single pair aviary birds, or a mixed collection in a very large

Queen Whydah. The courting rituals of all whydahs are very interesting. The male displays by making use of his long tail in ribbon-like flutterings during frequent skyward soars and rapid returns.

## FAMILY ESTRILDIDAE

It is from the many Estrildids that the hobby of foreign finch keeping derives an onward momentum. The birds of this family are often extremely colorful and of a small size. Many are well established in captivity. They make fine exhibition birds and are modest in price when compared with other popular bird groups, such as the parrots or the softbilled birds.

All members prefer a domed basket type nesting receptacle and their eggs are always white. Generally, both parents share the nest building and incubation duties. However, it is invariably the male that gathers material for the nest, while the hen normally does more eggsitting. The average incubation period is 12-14 days and the youngsters leave the nest at about 18-21 days of age. They are usually independent 12-16 days later. The Estrildids are commonly referred to by a number of collective names

Fire Finch. Fire Finches are not very long lived birds, about three or four years being their average allotted span. They generally get on well with other small birds, but some males prove to be vicious to others of their own kind.

aviary, they make excellent occupants. Most are hardy and long lived and tend to have a very specialized group of devotees. Some have quite a sweet song. They vary from reliable to very difficult when establishing as breeding birds. Specimen examples make attractive exhibition birds. Those species native to Britain or the USA require closed leg bands to establish that they were bred in captivity. A number of the species are very colorful, but those with much red in the plumage tend to fade in color when kept under captive conditions unless properly fed.

that are applied to a group of species within the family. These

livefoods in the diet during the breeding period. When

Zebra Finch. Other mutations of the Zebra Finch are still considered rare, but are becoming more available all the time. Some examples are: Chestnut Flanked, Pied, Fawn, Cinnamon. and Cream.

include waxbills, grassfinches, parrot finches, munias, and mannikins. Quite a number of the species are sexually dimorphic, which makes obtaining true pairs much easier. Most will make peaceful inhabitants in a mixed aviary, given that it is not overcrowded. Many are very hardy once acclimatized, others require background heat during the colder months. In all instances what you must safeguard against is the risk of birds being left out in a flight when there is likely to be a hard frost. Most will benefit from

pur-chasing those in which the sexes are similar you are advised to obtain three or more so that your chances of obtaining at least one true pair is increased. Once you have identified the sexes, place different colored celluloid split rings on the males and hens so that they can be easily identified in the future. The non ringed birds will thus be those in which the sex has not yet been established.

**The Pytilias Genus *Pytilia* 13cm (5in)**

There are just four Pytilias and they are best described as attractive rather than splendid in their colors. They are

African in distribution. Each has barred under parts, and a red tail and rump. The Melba Finch, *P.melba*, is possibly the best known of the four: it is also known as the Green-Winged Pytilia. It sports a red beak and red around its forehead and throat. The nape of the neck is gray and the body brown-green. The Melba settles well in an aviary but can be rather aggressive with smaller finches. It should be wintered indoors because it is not as hardy as its size might suggest. The Aurora Finch, *P.phoenicoptera*, is similar to the Melba but lacks the red beak and the red on the head. It is perhaps a little less aggressive than the Melba, but much depends upon the size of the aviary, number of occupants, and the individual character of the birds. This species is also called the Red-Winged Pytilia.

**The Twinspots Various Genera 13cm (5in)**

This group of six species is so named for the white spots that are seen on its under parts. Red is a feature of the plumage along with gray, black, and brown. The beak is black. Possibly the most well known of the group is Peter's Twinspot, *Hypargos niveoguttatus*. With its deep

Typical Show Cage. Show cages of this type are often used for Zebra Finches. This particular cage is not quite finished. It must be painted; usually black exterior and white or pastel interior.

red face and throat, black under parts spotted in white, brown body, and whitish eye ring, it is a most beautiful bird. The hen lacks much of the facial red and is rather dull. The Twinspots are delicate birds, and should never be left in an aviary over winter. The birdroom should be protected at a minimum of about 45°F (8°C) if they are to be kept. None of these birds are of low cost due to the small numbers imported. Others that may be seen in petshops or on dealer's lists are the Green-backed, *Mandingoa nitidula*, and more rarely Dybowski's, *Cytospiza dybowskii*. This latter species sports a gray-black head.

You are advised not to take on these species until you have gained some experience with hardier finches.

**The Fire Finches Genus**
*Lagonosticta* **to 13cm (5in)**
These little African waxbills comprise ten species, but only two or three are imported on a regular basis. Easily the most popular, and most modestly priced, is the Senegal Fire Finch, *L. senegala*. It is also known as the Common or Red-Billed Fire Finch. The face,

beak, rump and chest are red. The tail is black and the body brown. There are faint white spots on the under parts. The hen is altogether dull. This species is small yet quite hardy, and has been wintered outdoors in temperate climates, however, it would be prudent to keep them indoors with low background heat during the coldest months rather than take unnecessary risks.

The Fire Finches are happy little birds that mix well in an aviary. They also settle down, once acclimatized, to breed without undue problems if livefoods are readily available.

**The Cordon Bleus Genus**
*Uraeginthus* **13cm (5in)**
Cordon Bleus are named so for the extensive amount of blue in the plumage. There are three species, which at least in the males are easily differentiated. The Red-Cheeked, *U. bengalus*, sports red cheek bars and the blue extends from the side of the abdomen onto the chest and face. The tail is blue and the rest of the plumage brown. The Blue-Breasted, *U. angolensis*, lacks the red bars, while the Blue-Capped, *U. cyanocephalus*,

**Opposite page:** Bullfinch. A favorite among bird lovers because of its size and beautifully colored plumage. Bullfinches kept in captivity must be fed the proper diet otherwise they will quickly deteriorate.

has the entire head to the neck in blue. The hens of all three species are rather similar making positive distinction between them, and species variation, difficult. The Cordon Bleu can be a reliable breeder if ample livefood is available. All three are rather delicate when first imported and are best wintered indoors at all times. They are peaceful birds in a mixed aviary and can be recommended to the novice birdkeeper.

**Violet Eared Waxbill *Granatina granatina* 10cm (4in)**

   With violet cheek patches, blue forehead bar, black throat patch, red beak, and blue rump, the Violet Eared is an eye catching bird that could easily tempt one to purchase it. Avoid such an action because the species is highly insectivorous, very

quarrelsome in mixed company, and difficult to breed. It is also very delicate in temperate climates. Once experienced, however, it should be considered especially if planning to exhibit because these birds are astonishing.

**Lavender Waxbill *Estrilda caerulescens* 11.5cm (4.5in)**

   This little African waxbill is a firm favorite with birdkeepers and can be recommended to the beginner. The color is basically a steel gray with a red rump and tail. The beak is a dark crimson red-black. The sexes are similar, which is true of most members of the genus *Estrilda*. Once acclimatized this species can be a very reliable breeder, and at a modest price. It is quite hardy but should be wintered indoors. They can

Baby Blue Headed Parrot Finch. Young Parrot Finches have phosphor-escent spots at the corners of their beaks until they are weaned.

be allowed into the aviary during the warmer parts of winter days, or you can clad the aviary to protect it from severe frosts.

**Red Eared Waxbill**
*Estrilda troglodytes*
**10cm (4in)**
This African waxbill's most distinctive features are the vivid red wax like bill (for which the waxbills are named) and the red ear flashes that extend from the beak. The rest of the plumage is brown turning pinkish on the under parts. These birds seem to maintain their feathers in quite immaculate condition.

A somewhat similar bird is the Orange Cheeked Waxbill, *E. melpoda.* They have large orange patches on their cheeks. It is a little more nervous than the Red Eared Waxbill.

Looking much more similar to the Red Eared Waxbill is the Common or St. Helena Waxbill, *E. astrild.* This bird has red ear patches but the plumage is otherwise shades of gray and gray-brown with barring on the

Dark Fire Finch. The Dark Fire Finch is one of the more uncommon species of Fire Finches. All of the species appreciate being fed livefood during the nesting season.

under parts and wavy black lines on the wings and body. Like so many of the low priced African finches, more breeders are now turning their efforts to breeding. The St. Helena is possibly the easiest to achieve this with.

**Red Avadavat or Munia**
*Amandava amandava* **10cm (4in)**
This little waxbill is also known as the Tiger Finch and the Bombay Avadavat. It is well recommended to the beginner because it is hardy once acclimatized. Some are even kept in unheated housing over the winter. Unusually for the waxbills, the males exhibit

eclipse plumage and look like hens out of breeding condition. The full color males have red, speckled with black, on their heads, chest, and tail coverts. The wings, chest, and tail coverts are also speckled with white spots giving them a most pleasant appearance. The beak is red. The hen is altogether more plain, but does have some white spots. The Red Avadavat is a good mixer in a community aviary and has a pleasant voice. It is more expensive than the popular African Waxbills, and represents good value. The Green Avadavat, or

Munia, *A. formosa*, is much less of a proposition for the beginner. It is mostly shades of an olive-yellow type green. It is a difficult bird to breed, and is also more delicate than its red cousin.

**Gold Breasted Waxbill** *Estrilda subflava* **9cm (3.5in)**
     This gorgeous little waxbill is one of the smallest birds that can be kept in a cage or aviary (a fact that should be remembered when choosing aviary netting hole size). It is also called the Zebra or Orange Breasted Waxbill. It has

Black Headed Lady Gouldian Finch. The male of this species is the more beautiful of the sexes. Females are duller and paler editions of the male.

proved to be very hardy and an excellent mixer in a community aviary. Its size belies its toughness, but the author suggests providing it with background heating or indoor housing during the winter.

The male has a red stripe above the eyes, the breast is orange-yellow with black bars to the sides of under parts. The lower rump and tail coverts are red. The beak is also red. The hen is similar but paler and lacks the red eye stripe. Once settled into an aviary this species readily breeds. It is a low cost and well recommended bird.

### Zebra Finch *P oephila castanotis* 10cm (4in)

No finch is kept in greater numbers, nor has introduced more people to this group of birds, than the ever-famous Australian grassfinch, the Zebra Finch. It has much to recommend. Hardy, attractive, easily fed, easy to breed, extremely peaceful in a community aviary, and an excellent foster bird. It is chirpy, and active, very low priced in its wild coloration, and is seen in many color mutations as well as in a crested form. It is now regarded as a fully domesticated species. What more could one ask from

such a little bird! The normal or wild type colors are gray body with fawn-white spotted flanks. The chest has a black patch, flanked by gray barred white, which extends to the red beak. The tail is black barred with white. The male sports large orange cheek patches which are absent in the hen. Two horizontal black facial stripes enclosing white complete the bird. Mutations include the albino, the white, the chestnut-flanked white, the pied, and the fawn. The Zebra Finch requires no livefoods to rear chicks but commercial softfoods would be beneficial to offer. It is

Spice Finch. Spice Finches are often kept successfully with larger birds such as Java Rice Birds and many Weavers. They are usually very peaceful but a few individuals do become aggressive when in the company of smaller finches.

the ease of breeding these birds that is largely responsible for the false notion that all other finches will breed on a basic seed diet. It uses most types of nest receptacles, but the open fronted wooden box is often popular. The Zebra Finch is a highly popular exhibition bird. If a fault must be named, it is that they are so keen to rear chicks that they try to help other species raise their youngsters, which is not often appreciated! The Zebra should be regarded as an obligatory species for any beginner's aviary.

**Gouldian Finch** *Poephila gouldiae* **13cm (5in)**

If the Zebra Finch is the most popular Australian finch the Gouldian is certainly the most glamorous. With its black, red, or yellow head, its vivid purple chest and yellow underparts, each neatly separated by an almost straight line. There is also black and lilac in the plumage, and the beak is horn tipped pink-red. A few stunning color mutations are also available to make this one of the most desirable finches one could wish to own. Of course, these birds run considerably more expensive than your average finch, but they are certainly worth the cost. They are good mixers in a communal aviary, but are rather difficult to breed. Many are poor parents, and services of the Bengalese Finches are often used to rear the chicks and increase the number of eggs laid per season.

**Other Australian Grassfinches**

Space does not permit discussion of the numerous other finches of Australia but a few can be mentioned. All are considered more costly, but as such they represent good breeding investments. Any that are found on the market have been bred under captive conditions (unless you live in Australia). The Bicheno, or Owl Finch, *Poephila bichenovii*, with its white face edged with dark brown, is the smallest of the grassfinches and always attracts attention when seen. Its is a good mixer, but best bred in its own aviary.

The Star Finch, *Peophila ruficauda*, breeds readily. It sports a red face spotted with white, the latter extending to its chest and flanks. The species is quite bold and settles to new housing quite rapidly. The Cherry Finch, *Aidemosyne modesta*, is plain by

**Opposite page:** White Java Rice Bird. The White Java Rice Bird is completely white except for the rose, red, and pink found in the beak, eye ring, feet, and legs.

Australian finch standards being brown with white spots and bars. However, it is extremely placid which makes it a fine candidate for the community aviary. The Longtailed Grassfinch is a very elegant bird with a yellow beak, gray head with black throat patch, and soft brown body feathers. The red billed subspecies is known as Heck's Grassfinch. Although both are reliable breeders, they are best housed in their own aviary because of assertive tendencies.

The Australian finches are very worthy of specialized breeding as a group, and of course they make superb exhibition birds.

**African Silverbill** *Lonchura cantans* **11.5cm (4.5in)**

This rather plain colored little finch makes a first class addition to the mixed aviary. It is quite inoffensive and readily nests. It is a low cost species and its relative the Indian Silverbill, *L. malabarica*, is likewise. They do not require livefoods in order to breed. Well recommended. The Gray-Headed Silverbill, *L. griseicapilla*, is less common but more attractive.

**The Nuns Genus** *Lonchura* **12.5cm (4.5in)**

These popular mannikins or munias are but a few of the many species in this

Finch Nestbox. A nestbox of this type is normally used in a finch aviary. It not only serves the breeding purposes, but acts as a shelter as well.

Strawberry Finch. The male of this species has the most pleasant singing voices of all finches. They are very good aviary birds for they are peaceful, hardy, and relatively inexpensive.

genus. The Black-Hooded Nun, *L. ferruginosa*, has a black mantle and a brown body—not perhaps the most striking of colors, but nonetheless, very smart looking finch whose plumage always seems to be immaculate. They are inexpensive birds and can be encouraged to breed with bamboo plants included in the aviary. They also breed on a colony basis, which is useful because sexing the nuns is not possible from appearance. The nuns are peaceful aviary inhabitants and do not interfere or bully other finches.

Closely related to this species is the nominate form, the Tri-Colored Nun, *L. malacca*, which has white underparts. The White Headed Nun, *L. maja*, makes up a trio of these recommended birds.

As the name suggests it has a white mantle over a dark brown body. Another member of the genus that is frequently available is the Spice Finch, *L. punculata*, with its brown head and body over white scalloped underparts. Like most of the genus members it is a hardy species once acclimatized.

**Bengalese *Lonchura domestica* 10cm (4in)**

This highly popular and low cost finch is thought to be the domesticated form of the White Backed Munia, *L. striata*. It is seen in many color forms including white, albino, fawn, chocolate, and pied. The latter, if well marked, are most attractive in their shades of brown and white. Needless to say this finch is very popular with exhibitors, but it is also used as a foster parent for many species, notably the Gouldian Finch. Bengalese are excellent breeding birds who often have large clutches. Like the Zebra Finch, all first time aviary owners should include these easy to care for birds in their collection.

### Java Rice Bird *Padda oryzivora* 13cm (5in)

This species with its immaculate plumage, is not only a very distinctive bird, but also a standard favorite with foreign birdkeepers. Its cap is black over white cheek patches. The beak is red and the rest of the plumage is a soft gray becoming very light on the underparts. Also known as the Paddy Rice Bird, the Java is also seen in white, fawn, and pied mutations. The Java is a hardy and long-lived species, and one that is well able to look after itself in mixed company. They are not

found to be overly aggressive towards smaller finches, but it is wise to pick their aviary cohabitants with care, especially if the aviary is only of moderate size. Choose assertive companions, such as the weavers and large finches.

### Cutthroat *Amadina fasciata* 13cm (5in)

This species is so named for the vivid red stripe that encircles its throat. The hen lacks this. The rest of the plumage is shades of brown liberally marked with black flecks. It is also known as the Ribbon Finch. Like the Java, this species is hardy and able to defend itself from aggressive cohabitants in a mixed aviary should they try to interfere with it. When breeding it can be disruptive to smaller finches. It is a low cost species that invariably is found in the beginner's aviary in company with the

Nest of Shafttail babies 3 days old. Shafttails are ideal breeders although conditions must favor them before they will show much interest.

likes of diamond doves, cockatiels and selected hardy finches. The Cutthroat is a reliable breeder and only its low resale value restricts the numbers that are bred.

**FAMILY PLOCEIDAE**

This family comprises weavers and whydahs, a number of whom are parasitic on other birds. The whydahs lay their eggs in the nests of other species, such as certain waxbills, and leave these birds to rear their chicks. From an avicultural viewpoint parasitic whydahs are difficult to breed because they must have a host species present and breeding. However, they are popular as exhibition birds due to the gorgeous nuptial plumage of the male. Some are best kept in breeding groups, others are better paired in their own aviary. In all cases, it is advised only to mix them with birds of similar size. Availability is variable, and cost likewise, though as a group they are generally more costly than the waxbills. The non parasitic members of the family, such as the weavers, build intricate nests and some

Crimson Finch. The Crimson Finch is also known as the Australian Fire Finch. It is a very bullish bird that must be kept with larger, aggressive birds because of its behavior.

are polygamous.

The family also includes very many sparrows, and a number of these are at low costs. They may often be commonly sold under names that do not suggest they are sparrows. One or more popular examples of each type is given.

**Senegal Combassou**
*Hypochera chalybeata* **11.5cm (4.5in)**

The male is blue-black with a white or pink-red beak and red legs. It is parasitic on waxbills of the genus *Lagonostricta*, but is capable of rearing its own chicks. Unlike other whydahs, the Combassou does not feature long tail feathers. The hen and out of color males are rather plain shades of brown.

**Pintailed Whydah** *Vidua macroura* **13cm (5in)**

This commonly available species is brood parasitic on waxbills of the genus *Estrilda*. The male, in full color, sports a black cap, white throat and underparts, and black body. The beak is red. The nuptial tail feathers can be up to 25cm (10in) long. This is a hardy and long-lived little bird, but it can be rather disruptive in a mixed aviary of finches, being somewhat pugnacious. This does not encourage its host species to nest under confined situations. It is best to run 3-4 hens to one male as well as 2-3 pairs of the host.

There are numerous other very attractive whydahs, such as the Queen and the Paradise, but these are parasitic on species such as the Violet Eared Waxbill and the Purple Grenadier, which are themselves rather expensive and not recommended for the beginner. Breeding whydahs is very difficult and especially so with the non-parasitical species, such as the Yellow Backed Whydah, or Jackson's Whydah.

**The Bishops Genus Euplectes 15cm (6in)**

The bishops are a group of weaver birds that have long been popular due to the highly colorful plumage of the male during breeding season. Out

Zebra Finch. Not only is the Zebra Finch very attractive, but it also is the easiest to breed. Zebra Finches go merrily on producing clutch after clutch of young while other birds stand by observing.

is contrasted with yellow that extends higher onto the crown than in its orange relative. It also lacks

of color, the males and females are rather sober birds of shades of brown. These birds are polygamous, so the best breeding outcomes arise when 2-4 hens are paired with a single male. He builds a nest for each of the hens, but takes no part in incubation duties. If only a pair of bishops are housed together the male unduly harasses the hen, therefore single pairs are not advised. Bishops in full color are very stunning exhibition birds. The Orange or Red Bishop, *E.orix*, is so named because of the collar of fluffed feathers around the neck. Its head and underparts are black, while the chest, neck, and tail feathers are orange-red. The beak is usually black, in the male and horn-colored in the hen. The Napoleon Weaver, or Yellow, or Golden Bishop, *E. afer*, also has basic black plumage, but here it

the fluffed collar. There are in all approximately eight bishop species all of whom are variations of the theme of the two discussed.

**Sudan Golden Sparrow**
***Auripaser luteus* 13cm (5in)**
Often called the Golden Song Sparrow, however, these birds do not make melodious additions to your collection. The male has the head, chest, and underparts in yellow, the body is basically brown, and the beak is horn-colored, but, becomes black during breeding. The hen is mainly brown with some yellow on the head and body. These birds are inexpensive and are best bred in a colony system, or in a well planted aviary. They are quite hardy once acclimatized.

Pied Java Rice Bird. The most attractive Pied Java Rice Bird is one that is nearly equal in its division of colors (symmetrical). The Pied Java is a result of a mutation in captivity.

# INDEX